too cute
Kittens

TOO CUTE KITTENS

ISBN-13: 978-0-373-89287-7

Library of Congress Cataloging-in-Publication Data

Too cute kittens / Animal Planet's most impossibly adorable kittens
   pages cm
  ISBN 978-0-373-89287-7 (hardback)
1. Kittens--Pictorial works. 2. Kittens--Miscellanea. 3. Cat breeds--Pictorial works.
I. Animal Planet (Television network)
  SF446T66 2013
  636.8'07--dc23

2013024778

www.Harlequin.com
Printed in U.S.A.

too cute Kittens

Animal Planet's Most
Impossibly Adorable Kittens

too cute Kittens

Kyra Lee, a **RagaMuffin** cat, needs all the rest and relaxation she can get. Her four adorable and very active kittens are keeping her moving.

The four RagaMuffin kittens have not even opened their eyes yet, but the littlest kitten, Otto, is already an adventurer. When he is done napping, nothing is going to hold him back!

Brandy is the only sister in the litter, and her brothers don't always let her play with them. But her human gives her plenty of special attention. It's impossible to resist lavishing love on a kitten with such a charming lounge act.

Affable and docile, RagaMuffins are not adept climbers. They would much rather keep a low profile. But not little Otto! He is the bravest kitten of his litter, defying all stereotypes and climbing to new heights.

Fluffy, cuddly RagaMuffins are descended from Ragdoll, Persian, Burmese and Angora cats. RagaMuffins by nature are relaxed and the kittens are growing up to be low-lying, loving, lap-hogging cats.

Although **Ocicats** look like miniature jungle cats (they especially resemble the spotted ocelots that they are named after) they are completely domestic. But don't tell that to Rex! This spunky kitten knows he's wildly adorable!

British Shorthairs are the most popular breed of cat in England and it's not hard to see why! Their gigantic eyes, adorably round faces and perfect smiles make them unbearably darling.

Things get dodgy when Brits have the run of the office.
Moose hasn't quite figured out how to answer client calls, but he knows how to keep the hotline warm.

One of these classy British Shorthair kittens will grow up to assist its mom working at a veterinary office. They will need to learn office skills, but for now they have their cute skills in the bag.

Pippa, sporting an elegant gray beret, has got it all! She has office skills, client skills and people skills. Everyone is certain she is the perfect cat for the job!

Tiny Dancer is an **Abyssinian,** an athletic sleek breed with origins in Africa.
The runt of the litter, she isn't quite big enough to dance yet,
but extra small treasures are even dearer.

The **Cornish Rex** were bred from a mutation found in Cornwall, England, in the 1950s. Sleepy Tofu may be a mutant, but he sure is a cuddly one!

These five Cornish Rex kittens are only four days old, but won't get much furrier. The short downy coat they are born with is said to be the softest of all cat breeds and a special kind of cute.

Timber, the German Shepherd,
may be surrounded by what looks
like a pack of pointy-eared prowlers,
but they're all just cozy kittens to her.

Cornish Rex are named after the Astrex rabbit, which has a similar short wavy coat. Although, these kittens are more like sleeping beauties than hurried hares.

There is no cozier spot for Tofu's nap than with his friend Timber.
When you don't have much fur, you find it where you can.

The Cornish Rex come in all colors, patterns and playful personalities. Whatever their hue, they are as delightful as they are darling.

Tofu is five weeks old and eventually his body will catch up with his oversize ears, but in the meantime, he is keeping an ear out for new friends and his forever home.

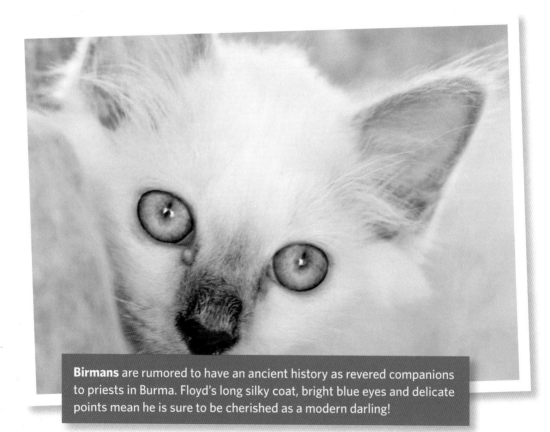

Birmans are rumored to have an ancient history as revered companions to priests in Burma. Floyd's long silky coat, bright blue eyes and delicate points mean he is sure to be cherished as a modern darling!

Cheetah is a **Savannah**, a breed created by crossing a domestic cat with the wild serval. He may look well behaved and innocent, but he's already on the prowl.

Toys are not just for fun, they are prey, and Cheetah's sister Cougar has her eye on the next "victim." No doubt she'll subdue it with one enthusiastic pounce.

Cougar's Cleopatra-style eyeliner is actually the mark of a hunter, helping to cut sun glare while she stalks.

Savannahs are considered to be friendly and social cats. Tiger can't wait to spend time with her new family, who is sure to think she is wildly captivating.

Burmese cats once roamed the palaces and temples of Burma, but Pepper doesn't need to roam any farther than the couch to demonstrate her charm and ability to coax you into a cuddle.

Munchkins were bred in the 1980s from a mutation of stubby-legged cats. These cats may be small in stature, but Stretch proves they are larger than the average cat in cute!

Not all Munchkin kittens are born with short legs. These kittens model their long limbs, proving that statuesque can also be adorably fashionable.

Munchkins are outgoing and playful cats that are simply irresistible. Stretch is looking extra huggable today!

Porkchop and Nugget prove that all good things are more delightful in pairs. So this sweet set of shorties sticks together.

Munchkins come in a mixed bag of coat colors that are either silky and long or plush and short. With such a wide variety of possibilities, these cuties are sure to find the perfect families.

When everyone is looking at your legs, you may as well strut with them. Stretch demonstrates his best charming, on-the-catwalk sashay.

Even though they are closer to the ground, short-legged Munchkins are fast, active and can even jump quite high. Nugget may be vertically challenged, but she will leap right into your heart.

Maine Coons with their thick coats and snowshoe paws are always ready to keep you warm. They hit the U.S. shores from France over 200 years ago and have been romancing us ever since.

Orange cats, even Maine Coons
like Dante, are four times more likely
to be male. And Dante is four times
more likely to be lovable.

Zack's mom is a **Calico**, a Domestic Shorthair with a tricolor coat. Calicoes are almost always female, so Zack doesn't look much like her, but he makes up for it in looking extremely pettable.

The **Domestic Shorthair** is the most popular cat in America. A wide mix of colorful characters, these felines make up 95% of all pet cats. When it comes to cute, they've got the market covered!

Twins Boots and Little Bear are exploring their personal wilds and bringing a dose of delightful to the domestic jungle.

Little Bear is five weeks old and has tucked himself deep into the domestic outback while he waits for a new jungle where as king, he can rule with a cherished paw.

Himalayans are a loyal lap cat. Handsome, fluffy and cloud-white, Jacques is waiting for the perfect lap to while away his days.

Russian Blues have silver-blue coats and a mysterious history. They are said to have been companions to Russian czars. It's no mystery, however, that Sputnik is perfectly precious.

Sputnik is definitely an innerspace traveler and his first unexplored space is going to be the ground floor (when he figures out how to use the stairs).

Sputnik, along with his brother and two sisters, may have just recently opened their eyes and discovered their legs, but they are already experts at sweet sibling siestas.

Russian Blues are lean, elegant, smart cats that make wonderful family pets. You only have to take one look at this precious pile of royal fur to know they are blue-blooded.

When Sputnik finally makes it downstairs, he discovers a world filled with wonders.
Whatever new friends this fearless explorer discovers, they are sure to be captivated by his regal charm.

Of all the household wonders to be found, the kitchen is truly a kitten's paradise, always filled with unexpected treasures.

Eventually, Sputnik runs out of new territory to explore, but the exploits are not over. The best adventure is yet to come....

The **Sphinx** was bred from a type of cat with a natural mutation discovered in 1966. Completely bald, this breed's fans are enchanted by their irresistible personalities and a very different kind of lovable.

Sphinx cats, like Gremlin, have to be kept in a climate-controlled environment to stay warm when they are young. The kittens may take extra care, but beauty has a price, and bald is beautiful!

Sphinx cats come in two varieties, straight- and curl-eared. The cats with curled ears are called elfs and Gremlin is adorably elfin.

Siberians are the national cat of Russia, and although they come in a variety of colors, all have a lush, dense, three-layer coat. Although these short-coated kittens have a Siberian mother, they also look an awful lot like the handsome cat next door....

Socks and Mittens have a family who is anxious to adopt them. They may not look like Russian highborns, but they are undeniably enchanting.

If Socks inherits his mother's build, he will be a large cat. Siberians are big, yet agile, felines, perfect for leaping up on the bed and keeping your spot warm.

These **Tabby** kittens were orphaned when they were only a few weeks old. But they were fortunate enough to find their way into a loving home where they met their new friend Nellie, a three-week-old orphaned skunk.

Singapuras are adaptable, spry cats that are big on climbing and jumping. Basil was the first of his litter to open his eyes, but Pepper and Saffron are right behind him and will soon be ready to leap into the new world.

It's not difficult to see where the Singapura kittens got their grace and good looks. Mom, Jasmine, is a feline charmer.

At five weeks old, the city Singapuras are all about stalking and catching prey. Toys are fun, especially when you can play with your siblings.

Saffron has learned that the best way to get attention is to stay out of trouble. She's looking for a quiet place and a cuddle.

Basil is always looking for more fun and adventure. It doesn't get much better than a tiny tunnel and an unexpected toy at the end.

These miniature athletes can't resist leaping to new heights.
Basil may be small in stature but the high jump is second nature!

Warm and trusting, **Ragdolls** are a breed that is always ready to melt into any loving lap. Bold Snowball is ready to find the perfect lap and stay forever.

The **Tonkinese** is a cross between Burmese and Siamese cats,
making the Tonkinese a breed with a charming sense of play and a chatty demeanor.

Queenie is a first-time mother with plenty of love to give. Tonkinese are born with white coats that darken over time, so it won't be long until her classy kittens have their mom's good looks.

These kittens have spent weeks getting up to no good in the best way possible. Now it's time to go to their forever homes. They are sure to go to families that think they are the cat's pajamas.

Tabby cats usually have striped coats and white socks. Although their coats can vary, they all have the letter "M" on their forehead, which is said to stand for "mao," Chinese for *cat*.

Muffin has two girls and two boys in her litter, an even mix of lovable. At four weeks old, the kittens know every comfortable position for napping and exactly how to be a perfect puzzle of precious.

Max is a classic Tabby with a love of climbing. He may be little, but he's already a leaping legend.

Paws likes his feet on the ground and is not too sure about climbing. All the same, he's willing to follow in Max's footsteps.

A little bit of adventure goes a long way for Paws. Staying on Max's tail has worn him out, but fortunately with three siblings, there is always someone willing to take a snooze.

Paws is a homebody and too irresistible not to keep. Even though he has plenty of suitors, he stays with Mom when his siblings find new homes. Who could say "no" to a face so sweet?

Exotic Shorthairs have the flat, round face of Persians with the short but luxurious coat of an American Shorthair. Mia is as darling as they come, especially after having her coat primped by Mom.

The **Toyger** is as domestic as they come, but when you cross a Bengal Tabby and a Domestic Shorthair Tabby, you get a cat with an exotic tigerlike coat. All the same, these kittens are most at home in a living room jungle.

Sparky and Tanya may be toy tigers, but they don't like to go it alone. Even when they are on the prowl, these two are inseparable.

Toygers were bred to raise awareness for their endangered and distant cousin, the tiger. Tigers may be struggling in the wild, but a kitten as irresistible as Sparky is sure to have a comfortable life and a ready lap.

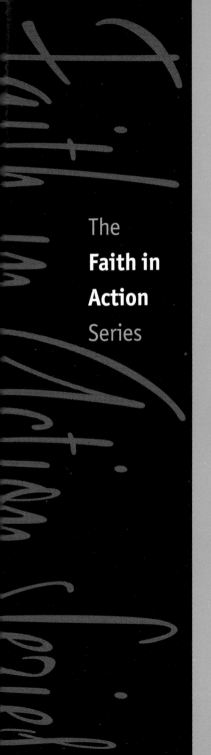

The
**Faith in
Action**
Series

A Pilgrimage
of Trust

··

The Story of Brother Roger
and Taizé

Liam Gearon

Illustrated by Brian Platt

RMEP

RELIGIOUS AND MORAL EDUCATION PRESS

A PILGRIMAGE OF TRUST

The Story of Brother Roger and Taizé

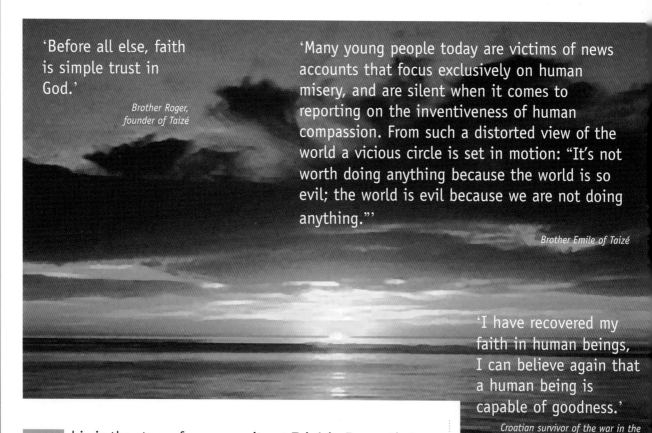

'Before all else, faith is simple trust in God.'

Brother Roger,
founder of Taizé

'Many young people today are victims of news accounts that focus exclusively on human misery, and are silent when it comes to reporting on the inventiveness of human compassion. From such a distorted view of the world a vicious circle is set in motion: "It's not worth doing anything because the world is so evil; the world is evil because we are not doing anything."'

Brother Emile of Taizé

'I have recovered my faith in human beings, I can believe again that a human being is capable of goodness.'

Croatian survivor of the war in the former Yugoslavia and visitor to Taizé

This is the story of a community at Taizé in France that has inspired such thoughts. It is a story of a young man who, over sixty years ago and in the middle of the Second World War, provided the space for quiet reflection and the search for meaning in a turbulent world where such things are difficult to find.

2

Taizé is famous the world over. Yet it is not fame or glory that the community wants. Indeed, the whole place is about taking space out from the world and making room for seeing things in a new light. Thousands flock to this part of France from all over the world all the year round. For most people who come to Taizé is a place of peace and a place of retreat. Even if it is only a temporary retreat, the peace many visitors feel when they leave can last for a very long time.

What Do You Think?

Important: In answering 'What Do You Think?' questions in this book, it is important that you not only state your opinion but also give as many reasons as possible for your opinion.

1. Why do so many news reports in the media focus on human misery? How do news reports affect your view of the world?

2. Do you agree that 'It's not worth doing anything because the world is so evil; the world is evil because we are not doing anything'?

3. Re-read the quote in the question above. It's an example of what's known as a 'vicious circle'. Can you think of another example? Can humankind ever break out of vicious circles?

A Land in Fear

In 1940, Taizé was far from at peace. The Second World War had started the year before and France, as it had been in the First World War, was on the front line of violence and terror. The Nazi forces of an invading German army had entered France in 1939. France had surrendered soon afterwards and the Germans occupied a large part of the country, mainly to the north.

The Germans were governed by a violent and intolerant political party called the Nazis. All over Europe the Nazis had built concentration and extermination camps to kill systematically anyone that opposed their way of thinking. The Nazis were particularly committed to killing all Jews and many other minorities – not only in Germany but in the whole of Europe, including France. The Germans took direct, political control of the northern part of France. But they allowed the southern part of France, known as 'Vichy France', to be governed by the French themselves. The so-called 'Vichy' government were as cruel as the Nazis. Basically the Vichy government did the Nazis' work for them in France, deporting many Jews and others to concentration camps or murdering them in France itself.

In 1940, a young man of twenty-five left Switzerland to travel to France, the country where his mother had been born. The man, named Roger, had recently recovered from tuberculosis (or TB), a life-threatening lung disease from which he'd suffered for many years. The situation in France and his own poor health made this journey full of risks. Staying in Switzerland, which remained neutral throughout the war, would have been much safer.

During his long, painful and weakening illness, however, Roger had discovered a vocation, a calling or sense of purpose to do something with his life. He was, after all, already twenty-five. The more he thought about it, the more he had a deepening sense of what his mission in life was. The idea he had might have seemed impossible, even slightly mad, but he felt this call was urgent and he must set off the moment he was fit enough.

The idea that had grasped him was to create a community that would set a small, personal example to a world at war, and more especially his homeland, France. This was to be a community where simplicity and service to others would be the key. The life of the community would be based upon the teachings of Jesus, Christian principles with love and kindness at their heart. This was in contrast to the world into which Roger had been born, where people who thought of themselves as Christians had fought and killed each other in millions on the battlefields of Europe during the First World War.

The slaughter of the First World War had ended only twenty years before. During that war, Roger's French grandmother had helped those in need on all sides of the conflict. When the Second World War started, Roger wanted to offer rapid help to anyone who needed it. In neutral Switzerland, he heard stories of hardship, brutality and persecution going on all over France, in both the northern part occupied by German forces and in Vichy France. So he decided to go to France at once.

One day, in this very dangerous environment, Roger was travelling in Burgundy, in the south east of France, on his way to Switzerland. He stopped at the old town of Cluny, well known all around the world for its ancient Benedictine monastery. The monks at Cluny had followed an extremely strict lifestyle, with much of their time spent in silence. The monastery had been destroyed in the 1790s, during the French Revolution, but the life the community had led appealed to Roger. It was then that he saw in the town an advertisement for a small house for sale. The house was in the village of Taizé and he walked through the Burgundy countryside to view it.

Taizé turned out to be a tiny village set in green and picturesque farmland. It consisted of only a few houses along a gentle slope leading to a small church built of local, sandy-coloured stone. Roger liked the look of the place. It was quiet and isolated. The house was in a bit of a mess, since it had been unoccupied for years, but it would make a perfect retreat. Here

he felt he could live the simple life that he sought.

Roger bought the house and moved in. First, he set about getting it into a state suitable to live in. There was no running water, so water had to be collected from the village well. It was a good way to meet the neighbours.

Taizé was in 'free' or Vichy France, close to the line that divided it from German Occupied France and about 100 km from the border with neutral Switzerland. It was thus well suited for another purpose. In this anonymous French village, no one suspected that the friendly man who had moved into the empty house was helping refugees escape from the Nazis. Roger was still sickly and weak as he had only just recovered from tuberculosis, but as his grandmother had helped the victims during the First World War, he was helping those of the Second.

Roger's sister, Genevieve, soon joined him in France. Their parents, still safe in Switzerland, were very worried. Their children were grown up but there were great dangers in helping refugees. Anyone caught working against the Nazis risked torture and execution. Roger and Genevieve's parents knew a retired French army officer and he secretly agreed to keep an eye on them.

Roger and Genevieve both had French backgrounds so there was no reason for anyone to suspect that they were any more than two innocent young people who had decided to return to their mother's homeland. Roger arranged for papers and transportation across the border for a number of refugees. We may never be sure how many but they included people whom the Nazis and their Vichy collaborators would have shot or sent to the death camps.

Soon, however, Roger himself was at risk. The neighbours knew his was a house of prayer. He was open about that, and very welcoming to all, but some of the people that appeared at his door were complete strangers. No one had seen or heard of them before. Did someone make a casual, unfortunate remark that brought suspicion on Roger? We do not know, but around 1942, Roger and his sister had to flee back to Switzerland. The French officer had done his job of secret protection by warning them that they were under suspicion from the Nazis.

Roger's grandmother inspired him in more than one way. She was a devout Protestant Christian, but she also saw religion as a force that could divide people instead of uniting them. She knew that the First World War was not in any sense a religious war, but divisions between Christians – often between Protestants and Roman Catholics – had led to wars in the past and were still a source of hostility. As a symbol of reconciliation between Christians, Roger's grandmother began to pray in Roman Catholic as well as Protestant churches, but she brought Roger up as a Protestant. During the time when Roger and Genevieve sheltered refugees, he prayed alone. He did not want to force his religious beliefs on anyone, perhaps especially those persecuted for their own religious or ethnic background.

What Do You Think?

1. Roger and Genevieve took a risk by helping refugees in wartime France. In what circumstances might you be prepared to risk danger? Why?

2. What might have given Roger such a strong sense of purpose for his life at this time?

Return to Taizé

In 1944, Roger was able to return to Taizé. This time he travelled without his sister, who remained in Switzerland. He had an idea to start a community rather like a monastery.

The war was not over but France was free. Although the fighting had stopped, living conditions in France remained difficult. The war had destroyed not only homes and factories but also farming and transport. Food and other essentials were in short supply. People, old and young, were suffering pain and grief. Many children had lost one or both parents. In post-War Taizé, Roger did what he could to help. He had not yet formed a community as such, but people in need of assistance would often drop by and stay at the house.

During the war, the French Resistance had taken enormous risks to undermine German power. Captured Resistance members had been tortured, often to death. Many Resistance fighters had been executed by the Nazis. Now that the Nazis had been defeated, many people in France were out for vengeance. Men and women who had collaborated with the occupying forces, or who had worked for the Vichy government, were themselves persecuted. In their thirst for revenge in the months immediately after the Nazi defeat, many people took the law into their own hands.

When a new French government was elected, many Nazi collaborators were prosecuted in French courts of law for crimes committed during the Vichy régime. Those who had committed serious atrocities like mass murder were executed. It was a time of bitterness and revenge. As a symbol of reconciliation, every Sunday Roger offered food and hospitality to defeated Germans held in a nearby prisoner-of-war camp.

1. Is revenge every justified? Give examples to support your answer.

2. After a war, should people accused of war crimes be tried in court? Why?/Why not? Think about (a) how difficult it might be to get a fair trial, (b) whether justice has to be seen to be done, (c) whether we need to 'forgive and forget' and move on.

A Simple Life

Although Roger did not actively encourage other people to join him at Taizé, they did. On Easter Sunday 1949, the small house became a formal community. It was not a monastery. It did not belong to any of the traditional groups like the Benedictines. But it was on this Easter Day that the group, who already called each other by the title 'brother', true to monastic tradition, agreed to a set of rules.

The brothers agreed to live a life of celibacy (abstaining from sexual relations) and poverty. Everything would be shared. No one would own anything personally. Just as important, this sharing was to be spiritual as well as material. One of the community's most important ideals was that life should be as simple as possible, so the prayers were simple. There were no ornate, complicated ceremonies. There were readings from the Bible, and much time for silent meditation.

Taizé began to grow. Others joined the first brothers. Within ten years, Taizé started also to attract increasing numbers of young people. From the 1950s and 1960s, these young people would visit from curiosity. They would make brief visits. They were often searching for meaning in their own lives. The word got around that this community in France offered something different. It was Christian but it was different. Young people went to find out how and why.

What they found was a community living like monks in a traditional monastery but more open and accessible to the visitors who wanted to share their experience without actually becoming brothers. A small number did want to commit their lives to Taizé but visitors were plentiful, and even the shortest stays in the community proved inspiring. Visits seemed to energise and refresh young people, who left ready to return to the challenges that they faced in the world.

Taizé today is still a male monastic organisation though there are nuns nearby with strong links. In the mid-1960s, members of an international religious group called the Sisters of St Andrew arrived in the village next to Taizé. Later they were joined by some Ursuline Sisters, from Poland. The brothers and sisters worked together in welcoming the visitors to Taizé.

Two things began to mark out Taizé as different from other Christian religious communities. First, its rules seemed more relaxed than those of most other monasteries and convents. Taizé seemed somehow freer. Its members were not separated from everyday life like they are in many convents and monasteries. Second, and even more noticeable, Taizé was open to Christians of all major denominations – Protestant, Roman Catholic and Orthodox. No other convent or monastery was like

A new brother promises to live by the rules of the community

it. These differences would later attract many young people to Taizé.

As these distinctive features of Taizé began to emerge, the Cold War was at its height. Europe was divided into 'Western Europe' and a Communist-controlled 'Eastern Bloc' led by the Soviet Union (USSR). In the West, governments were democratically elected and individuals had much greater freedom than those in the Eastern Bloc. Many families were divided because people living in the Eastern Bloc couldn't travel to Western Europe without special permission. The Communists also tried to suppress religion and in some Eastern Bloc countries the Bible was banned. From 1962 on, brothers from Taizé made secret journeys into Eastern Bloc countries.

It wasn't the sort of activity the average monk usually engaged in. Taizé brothers would often smuggle forbidden Christian literature to Christians who lived behind the so-called Iron Curtain. They didn't just bring books like the Bible, they also brought news of the outside world. And that news brought hope. It was a spirit of hope and freedom that would eventually bring down the Soviet Empire in the late 1980s. When the Soviet Union collapsed, many individuals from Eastern Bloc countries formerly under its control were able to visit Taizé themselves. They continue to do so today.

What Do You Think?

1. There are still countries in the world where it is illegal to give away or sell Bibles and they have to be smuggled in. Why do you think some governments might not wish Bibles to be available? Is there any book that you would risk smuggling into a country where people were not free to choose for themselves? Why?/Why not?

2. A famous lager advertised itself as 'reaching the parts that other beers do not reach'. But what sort of spiritual things feed human beings and reach the parts that ordinary foods don't reach?

3. Christianity has a long tradition of monasticism and retreat from the world. Why do you think this is known as the contemplative life? Do you think such a life has any value today? Do you think the Taizé experience could be a form of escapism?

A Church of Reconciliation

To the brothers of Taizé, simple Christian beliefs expressed by the gospels were what mattered. More and more, Taizé itself began to develop its thinking as an ecumenical community, one that welcomed Christians of all denominations – Roman Catholic, Orthodox and Protestant – as well as those for whom belief was far from easy or assured. The main gathering place for worship at Taizé was named the Church of Reconciliation to emphasise the wider mission of the community: to bring unity amongst Christians, and peace in the wider world.

The Taizé community today has more than a hundred brothers from various different Christian denominations and from all over the world. As the Taizé website says: 'By its very existence, the community is thus a concrete sign of reconciliation between divided Christians and separated peoples. The brothers live by their own work. They do not accept gifts or donations for themselves, not even their own personal inheritances, which are given by the community to the poor.'

Taizé village

With numbers increasing year by year, it became obvious that the community at Taizé would need a new church building to allow everyone to worship together, especially in the summer months, when up to five thousand pilgrims from over seventy-five nations have been known to make the journey to France. The Church of Reconciliation was extended in the 1970s in order to able to accommodate such increased numbers.

Whatever the numbers, the underlying principle has remained the same. The idea is that people can come to Taizé to take time out from the schedule of their daily lives, from their ambitions, and pray or just reflect about what really matters. It is a question of getting priorities right and thinking through how to put those priorities into action. So, what actually happens at Taizé?

Although life at Taizé is ordered, it retains a sense of freedom within its rules for living. Without any rules, even a community like Taizé might descend into chaos! The typical Taizé day has remained unchanged in years and the timetable will be like this:

8.15 a.m. **Morning prayer in the Church of Reconciliation**
Followed by a simple breakfast of French bread and hot chocolate

10.00 a.m. **Introduction to the day**
Group leaders give a very short lecture on the main themes.

11.00 a.m. **International Groups**
The chance for individuals from different countries of the world to share issues of political and religious importance to their regions

12.20 p.m. **Midday prayer in the Church of Reconciliation**
Followed by a simple lunch – in the summer, when visitors are in their thousands, queues are long!

2.00 p.m. **Optional song practice**
This is for those who want to share their musical talents or just practise the songs of Taizé that are used during the daily worship

3.30 p.m. **Practical work/small group discussion**
This will be according to the themes set for the week – often linked to Bible readings

5.00 p.m. **Snack**

5.30 p.m. **Meetings by country or by theme**
This is an opportunity to draw together any of the issues that have been raised during the day at the discussion or international groups

7.00 p.m.	**Supper**
8.30 p.m.	**Evening prayer followed by prayer vigil in the Church of Reconciliation**
	Followed by free time – people can meet informally in the café

13

Brothers and visitors pray and reflect together in the Church of Reconciliation

The group discussions might focus on issues such as 'Is forgiveness possible?', 'What kind of Europe do we want?', 'The challenge of globalisation', or topics related to art or music. There is an atmosphere of openness and listening which helps group members from different countries, cultures and Christian traditions to begin to understand each other and find 'roads' towards unity, trust and peace in today's divided world.

The highlights of each day are when the community and all those visiting Taizé gather for prayer and reflection. As in the early days, the pattern of worship is simple. At the beginning of each service, the members of the community arrive (not always at the same time) and sit down a long central aisle, marked by a row of green plants, something like a miniature hedgerow! There are no seats so everyone sits on the floor – all the brothers, including Brother Roger, with the congregation either side of the aisle. Although in the summer the gatherings are packed, there are still times, like mid-winter, when the number of guests is small and there is plenty of room in the enormous church.

The worship at Taizé has a number of special features. Perhaps the most distinctive is the music. Short prayers are sung to simple melodies. The songs are repeated again and again so that the meaning of the words sinks in, and everyone can take part in this time of prayer or 'meditative singing'. Another thing visitors will notice is the range of languages used, including English, French and German, but also Latin. The absence of seats is characteristic of the Eastern Orthodox Christian tradition, as are the large icons of Jesus and Mary and the saints that decorate the low, candlelit altar at the front of the Church of Reconciliation.

An essential feature of the worship is silence. A song or a Bible reading will cease and all of a sudden silence will descend. In more traditional Christian worship like Sunday services, silence will rarely last for more than a minute or so. At Taizé, the silence, and the contemplation (meditation) it encourages, expand, continuing for five, ten, even fifteen minutes. In those minutes, people somehow explore a depth within themselves. It is this experience that the community of Taizé can offer their guests.

What Do You Think?

1. Why do you think the church at Taizé is called the Church of Reconciliation?

2. If you had the opportunity to meet young people from anywhere in the world, which three countries or parts of the world would you choose? What three questions or issues would you like to discuss with them?

3. Would you welcome an opportunity to take time out to spend in peace and in silence? Why?/Why not?

A Pilgrimage of Trust

The growth of Taizé during the late 1960s and early 1970s occurred at a time when many people in the West no longer wanted anything to do with organised religion, particularly the Christian churches. Young people who had been brought up to be Christian felt there were now so many alternatives, a mood once caught by the phrase 'sex, drugs and rock 'n' roll'. The Christian churches seemed stuffy and old-fashioned.

Church leaders were worried and there was much discussion about how to make the message of Christianity relevant to the modern world. Between 1962 and 1965, for example, the Roman Catholic Church held a worldwide gathering, called the Second Vatican Council, to address this issue.

Brother Roger was influenced by this urgency of ensuring people didn't simply ignore Christianity, or reject it as completely irrelevant. He was particularly concerned with the needs of young people. They had, after all, found something appealing about the Taizé community since it began. They had started coming in the 1950s and now, in the late 1960s, they were still arriving, in hundreds, especially in the warm months of the Burgundy summer.

Brother Roger has defined Taizé's mission as a 'pilgrimage of trust'. Every year, as part of this pilgrimage of trust, he writes a letter that is sent to most parts of the world. This *Letter from Taizé* is translated into as many as sixty languages and 'postmarked' from wherever Brother Roger happens to be staying when he writes it. Also, at the end of every year, Taizé prepares a five-day 'European Meeting' which brings together up to a hundred thousand young people in one of the major cities of Eastern or Western Europe – Prague, London, Rome, Vienna or Paris, etc. This meeting is an opportunity to follow a 'Taizé lifestyle' in a different part of the world: the spirit of Taizé is about people not a place!

What Do You Think?

1. Why does Taizé attract so many young people?

2. Do you think their reasons for coming have changed since the 1950s? Why?/Why not?

3. From what you have read, how would you describe the spirit of Taizé?

16

…o the spirit of Taizé can be taken anywhere. And it's not just …bout prayer and the spiritual life. It's also a matter of …hristians feeling their responsibility for others, especially the …ess fortunate.

In the *Letter from Taizé* marking the new millennium, Brother …oger asked this question: 'Are there realities which make life …eautiful, and which can be said to bring a kind of inner joy?' …rother Roger's answer is implied in the question: 'Yes' is the …iven answer. 'And one of those realities bears the name of trust.' …o simple that, 'Even a child can do it'. The trust he refers to is …n God and in other people:

Trust does not cause us to forget the suffering of so many unfortunate people across the earth, those who have no work or nothing to eat.

These trials make us reflect: how can we be people who, sustained by a life of communion in God, take on responsibilities and search with others for ways of making the earth a better place to live in?

A trust that comes from the depths does not lead us to flee responsibilities, but rather to remain present in places where human societies are in turmoil or out of joint. It enables us to take risks, to keep going forward even in the face of failures.

And we are amazed to find that this trust makes us able to love with a selfless love, one that is not all possessive.

So the community at Taizé like to see themselves as a 'parable of community', a sort of model for how people from different backgrounds can get on together without fighting, working out their differences together. Taizé is living proof of a community that works and is a model for reconciliation in a world where communities are so often divided or troubled. This is why for over the past fifty years the brothers have gone to live in some of the world's most disadvantaged neighbourhoods – in Africa, Asia, Eastern Europe and South America.

The spirit of Taizé sees that even in rich countries people can suffer from a sort of spiritual poverty – loneliness, isolation and depression. But within rich countries there are also those who are physically extremely poor. Brother Roger and the members of the Taizé community have therefore also worked amongst the most disadvantaged people there. Brother Roger has lived with the destitute of New York's 'Hell's Kitchen', where Taizé brothers minister to the needs of some of the poorest of the poor in the world's richest country. He has stayed with the disadvantaged in India and in the Philippines. Brother Roger has stayed with native Indians in Chile and tribal peoples in many other parts of the world. He has visited areas torn by civil war like Haiti and Lebanon, and countries like South Africa where people have been divided by the colour of their skin. He has also lived in the most remote and inhospitable places of the earth like the Sahara Desert.

What Do You Think?

1. What experiences or aspects of life might bring a person an 'inner joy'?

2. What qualities might make a Taizé brother a suitable worker to help disadvantaged people? What qualities might the brother bring to situations away from Taizé itself? Would other social or aid workers share any of these qualities?

3. Is trusting others easy or hard? Give reasons or examples.

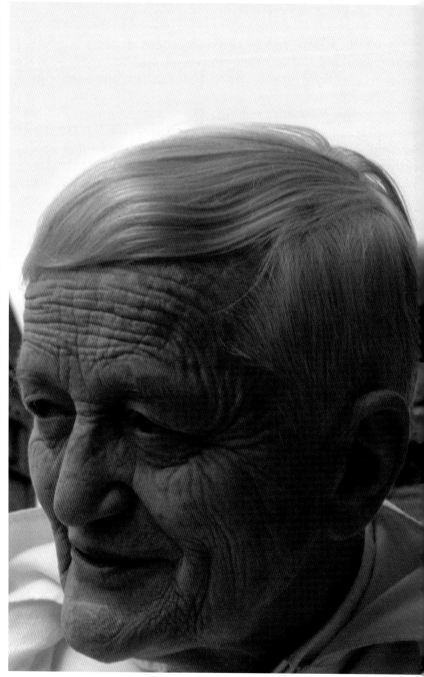

Brother Roger

A Beautiful Life

Brother Roger has not grown any less idealistic with age. Even now, as he approaches ninety, he stresses that Taizé's message is not something new. The Taizé message is simply the Christian message. He would say that all Taizé does is present to the world the teachings of the Gospel-writers, those who originally spread the message of Jesus after his death.

Brother Roger regards the message of the Gospels as a simple one, based upon love of God and love of one's neighbour. Sixty years after buying the small village house in Taizé, as the twentieth century drew to a close, he defined Taizé's expression of the Christian message by saying:

'Faith is a simple trust in God.'

What Taizé continues to demonstrate today is how this trust can be achieved. Anyone who has ever visited Taizé will tell you that the living conditions are very simple.

Taizé – the place itself – is, though, a place of temporary retreat. It is somewhere you can go for a while before returning to your home town or city or village refreshed. But its inspiration can have a long-lasting effect. Taizé encourages those who visit to take the spirit of renewal and reconciliation back to their own homes and their own communities. The message is one that for many people somehow makes life beautiful.

What Do You Think?

1. Why do people sometimes become less idealistic and even disillusioned with life as they grow older? Why has this not happened to Brother Roger?

2. Why do visits to Taizé have a long-lasting effect on some people's lives? Have you had any positive experiences like this?

3. For a religious believer, how important is trusting God? Can someone have faith in God without trusting God?

Biographical Notes

1915 Roger born in Switzerland.

1939 Beginning of Second World War. Nazi forces invade France and Germans occupy northern part of country. 'Vichy France', in the south, governed by French.

1940s Roger pays wartime visit to France. Discovers and buys house in the village of Taizé near the monastic town of Cluny. Lives simple life at Taizé with his sister Genevieve, also helping refugees escape from the Nazis.

1942 Roger and Genevieve in danger of arrest and return to Switzerland.

1944 France freed from Nazi occupation. Roger returns to Taizé.

1945 End of Second World War. Other people begin to join Roger at Taizé.

1949 On Easter Sunday the small house in Taizé becomes a formal community.

1950s–1960s Community grows, attracting ever larger numbers visitors, especially young people.

1962 and 1965 Second Vatican Council held by Roman Catholic Church. Discusses how to make Christian message relevant in modern world.

1970s Church of Reconciliation extended in order to accommodate increased numbers of international visitors to Taizé

1974 Brother Roger organises first worldwide meeting for young people.

1989 Collapse of the Soviet Union opens Taizé to many Eastern European Christians.

1980s–1990s Taizé brothers do increasing amounts of 'outreach' work – living and working with poor and oppressed people aroun the world.

2000 Brother Roger marks the new millennium with a special *Letter from Taizé*.

1 Imagine you have travelled to Taizé from any part of Europe. Write a diary entry describing your journey, how you feel now you have arrived at Taizé and your hopes for your visit OR do this on computer and paste in photos and other material that might go into a visitor's souvenir book.

2 Script or role play in pairs a conversation between two people who have returned from a visit to Taizé that they found (a) positive, inspiring and (b) negative, disappointing. How might they describe their different feelings and experiences?

3 Imagine you are a new Taizé brother. Write a letter to a friend or member of your family explaining why you joined the community, outlining your life at Taizé and how you feel now you're there.

4 Read Chapter 2 of the Acts of the Apostles in the Bible. (The first part of the chapter is about Pentecost, the last part of the chapter is about the early Christians sharing everything they had in common.) How far does life in the early Christian community as described there resemble life at Taizé today? What similarities and differences are there? Make a list in two columns.

5 Look up the Taizé website www.taize.fr. Create a world map of Taizé's 'outreach' activities around the world. Where is the nearest to you?

6 Imagine you are a Taizé brother who has left France to work 'out in the world'. Write a letter describing what you're doing and where, why you decided to leave Taizé and how you feel about your move.

7 In addition to prayer and contemplation, the Taizé message is about human solidarity. Look up the word 'solidarity' in a dictionary. What are the members of the Taizé community doing world wide to try to show this solidarity? Present your answers as a news report or chart including a definition of what you understand by 'human solidarity.'

8 One of the most famous sets of rules for community life was written by St Benedict in Italy fifteen hundred years ago.

(a) Find out about the life of St Benedict and the Benedictine community he founded. See if you can find a copy of the Rule of St Benedict. Are there any similarities between this approach to community life and that at Taizé?

(b) See what you can discover about Benedictine monastic communities in England, Wales, Scotland or Ireland. (For starters, try a search for Ampleforth Abbey (Yorkshire), Buckfast Abbey (Devon), Downside Abbey (Somerset) and Prinknash Abbey (Gloucestershire).) What similarities and differences are there between life there and at Taizé?

(c) Find out about some other sorts of Christian religious communities such as:

- the Iona community
- the Julian Meetings
- Coleg y Groes
- the Othona community
- Charney Manor
- St Cuthbert's Centre, Holy Island

(d) If you were offered the chance to visit one of the Christian communities you have researched, including Taizé, which would you choose and why?

9 Find out about religious communities (like Taizé) in other religious traditions such as Buddhism. Make a list of beliefs and practices in Buddhist or other religious groups and then compare them with those at Taizé.

10 Imagine you were to start a religious community.

(a) Brother Roger went to France to do this. Choose your own location for a new community: where would you go and why? (Try an internet search to check your first choice.)

(b) What would be the ideal number of people to bring? Why?

(c) What kind of rule would you establish? Make a list of ten of the most basic rules. Display the lists around your classroom and compare them. What similarities are there between the kinds of rules listed? What differences are there? What reasons can you suggest for these similarities and differences?

(d) Design a website for your community. Before you do this, look at what's on the Taizé website www.taize.fr. Think carefully about the image that your website will present to the world. What website link pages would you include?

11 Listen to some Taizé music (see www.taize.fr for available Taizé recordings). How does it make you feel? Why do you think the Taizé community have chosen this music for their worship? Why has some religious music like this (e.g. Gregorian chant) become popular among non-religious people in the twenty-first century? Do you think it's fair to take music written for a deeply spiritual purpose and just use it for relaxing listening? Why?/Why not?

12 Use poetry, music, art or dance to express the spirit of Taizé. Think of a key word or words or melody or a rhythm form.

13 The following statement reflects the community's idea about the purpose of visiting Taizé:

> Each person is invited, after his or her stay, to live out in their own situation what they have understood, with greater awareness of the inner life within them as well as of their bonds with many others who are involved in a similar search for what really matters.

Take some serious time to reflect and write about the things that are most important in your life.

14 On the Taizé website, you can find a number of links to India. But some states of India are becoming very difficult places in which to practise Christianity. Follow the links to Asia and India on the Human Rights Watch website www.hrw.org. (Human Rights Watch is an international, New York-based human rights organisation that campaigns for human rights around the world. Its Annual Reports are very reliable accounts of politics around the most troubled parts of the globe.) How can tolerance of other people's beliefs be promoted? Create a rap or a poster or a radio or TV advert that might try to do this. Why do you think some people are very intolerant of the beliefs and values of others?

15 Arrange a class debate with speakers for and against the motion:

> This House believes that if everyone could go to stay at Taizé for a few weeks, the world would be a better place.

16 (a) Research two or three issues that divide Christians today or have caused violent conflict in the past, e.g. views about the ordination of homosexual priests or of women priests or about worship, especially what churches refer to differently as the Eucharist, Mass, Communion, or the Lord's Supper. Why do you think some Christians feel so strongly about these issues?
(b) How does Taizé try to bring all Christians (and other people) together? How might a visit to Taizé help Christians of different denominations to move closer to each other or heal divisions in the Church?

A Pilgrimage of Trust

Religious and Moral Education Press
A division of SCM–Canterbury Press Ltd,
A wholly owned subsidiary of
Hymns Ancient & Modern Ltd
St Mary's Works, St Mary's Plain
Norwich, Norfolk NR3 3BH

First published 2004

ISBN 1 85175 323 0

Designed and typeset by
TOPICS – The Creative Partnership,
Exeter

Printed in Great Britain by
Brightsea Press, Exeter for
SCM–Canterbury Press Ltd, Norwich

Notes for Teachers

The first Faith in Action books were published in the late 1970s and the series has remained popular with both teachers and pupils. However, much in education has changed over the last twenty years, such as the development of both new examination syllabuses in Religious Studies and local agreed syllabuses for Religious Education which place more emphasis on pupils' own understanding, interpretation and evaluation of religious belief and practice, rather than a simple knowledge of events. This has encouraged us to amend the style of the Faith in Action Series to make it more suitable for today's classroom.

The aim is, as before, to tell the stories of people who have lived and acted according to their faith, but we have included alongside the main story questions which will encourage pupils to think about the reasons for the behaviour of our main characters and to empathise with the situations in which they found themselves. We hope that pupils will also be able to relate some of the issues in the stories to other issues in modern society, either in their own area or on a global scale.

The 'What Do You Think?' questions may be used for group or class discussion or for short written exercises. The 'Things to Do' at the end of the story include ideas for longer activities for RE or Citizenship and offer opportunities for assessment.

In line with current syllabus requirements, as Britain is a multifaith society, Faith in Action characters are selected from a variety of faith backgrounds and many of the questions may be answered from the perspective of more than one faith.

Acknowledgements
The publishers would like to express their sincere thanks to Catherine Bowness for the invaluable work she did in developing the Faith in Action Series during her five years as Series Editor (1997–2002) and to the Taizé Community for help with this book.

The publishers would also like to thank Terence Copley for his contribution to the editorial work on this book, particularly the questions and tasks for students.

All photos S. Leutenegger, copyright © Ateliers et Presses de Taizé, 71250 Taizé-Communauté, France.